Garden and Table

The Journal of Harald Bumbleburr

Stephanie Drummonds

and Daniel Myers

Cover background by
Runfang Zhang, Silkresource.com
Used with permission.

ISBN: 0692228861
ISBN-13: 978-0692228869

DEDICATION

For my family, who always have my back. And for my husband,
John, who is always by my side - Stephanie

For my mother, who taught me to cook because my older brothers
couldn't be trusted to make dinner properly - Daniel

CONTENTS

INTRODUCTION

The remnants of the journal of Harald Bumbleburr reproduced here were discovered quite by accident. They had languished for years, half-forgotten, in a dusty archive in Steeple which featured the collection of antiquarian Henry Ponsmore-Reid. In his lifetime, Ponsmore-Reid's character was somewhat tarnished by his propensity for excising the most decorative and elegant pages from historic manuscripts to sell as a way of supplementing his meager income. Following his death under mysterious circumstances, his widow and surviving children sought to rehabilitate his legacy by establishing a library with the remainders of his collection.

The journal, along with other books in similar incomplete condition or lacking in artistic value, was relegated to the bottom shelf of a back room, only coming to light during a doctoral candidate's research on the composition and importance of private libraries of the Victorian period. Even then, the journal's unusual culinary and cultural insights into the lives of Halflings were nearly overlooked because of its curious provenance.

The majority of the extant pieces of the manuscript were written in a neat, elegant script and appear to have been hand bound in rich burgundy leather. However, age and indifferent storage over the years have reduced the neat manuscript to a stack of assorted pages, loosely contained within the cracked and brittle leather covers. Given Ponsmore-Reid's reputation, it is also safe to assume that pages of greater interest might have been removed for separate sale, and may even now be safely locked away in private collections. There were also a number of separate pages tucked inside the journal which were obviously not part of the original text. Some were in a more hurried script, others in a different hand altogether, as though the author were collecting notes and recipes from friends and acquaintances. These were shoved haphazardly among the original pages, so it was difficult to determine where, if at all, these pages fit into the narrative structure of the journal.

Aside from his own words, there are few references in any of the contemporary records regarding Harald himself, which was totally appropriate for a gentleman of his age and standing. Records of his birth and death show that Harald Bumbleburr lived to the ripe age of 120, and as there are no mentions of marriage or children either in his journal or the historical records, it is presumed that he remained a lifelong bachelor.

Outside of his own writings, the greatest wealth of information comes from the proceedings of the East Riding Horticultural Society (ERHS), of which he was a long-standing member, even serving several terms as chairman. From the records, we can deduce that Harald was of middling height for a Halfling, solid but not overly plump and entirely ordinary in appearance – with one exception. Several entries in the minutes of the ERHS list comments, and complaints, about Harald's penchant for outlandish waistcoats.

He was apparently an enthusiastic and highly successful gardener, cultivating a large enough plot that he required an employee to assist him. He seems to have had little luck with these assistants, as both the journal and the ERHS minutes make note of several different names in that capacity.

Due to the fragmentary nature of the original source, we are obviously unable to reproduce the journal in its entirety. As a result, we have excerpted sections which seem most illustrative of the author's personality, interests and expertise both in the garden and the kitchen, as well as highlighting the Halfling love of meals – copious and often. Wherever possible, we have endeavored to maintain Harald's phrasing and discussions, his unique voice.

While the remaining text has no clear divisions, we have elected to separate the text by season, beginning with the Spring, the start of a Gardener's year. Each section will highlight the foods available and recipes utilized at the appropriate time of year. [NOTE: Specific gardening instructions incorporated herein are reproduced from the manuals of the ERHS, which were stored in the same archive.]

PART 1 - SPRING

"Greening Month" (April)

In the first part of Greening Month, bring forth and put out to air the lemon and orange trees and any other trees that have been shut up since the first frost. Plant olive and pomegranate trees and carefully prune others such as fig and chestnut.

Take time also to feed the pigeons in the fields, 'til the new growth be sufficient to feed them. Tend well the apiaries, cleaning the hives for the new honey to come.

~East Riding Horticultural Society Manual - Volume 1~

[Editor's note: from the context of both the journal and this manual, we can presume that the climate near Harald's home is similar to that of the portion of England where the manuscript was found. Given this similarity, citrus and olive trees would certainly have been imported, and would require careful wintering in a conservatory or hothouse.]

Greening Month, 3rd day
The sun was high and truly warm for the first time today. After a longer and harder than usual winter, I found myself itching to get out into my garden. Young Merwyn arrived early to clear the beds of their winter debris and stir the compost and was already hard at work when I came out after a hearty breakfast of toasty bread with gooseberry jam, roasted eggs and several rashers of bacon.

The feel of the moist earth between my toes, and the rich loamy smell of the compost worked on my nerves like a tonic. Each year I look forward to spring and the joy of adding the first new greens to the preserved fruits and vegetables which have graced my table through the winter months. Despite the late start to the season, I have high hopes for the garden this year.

By the time the sun was high, I was more than ready for my elevenses. Mistress Parton from down the road stopped by on her way to market. Her hens laid quite well this morning, so I was able to barter with her for a goodly number of eggs, which made up my mind on what to make.

I took three of the eggs, which were unusually large, and beat them well with snipped herbs from the pots in my kitchen window. I chopped an onion into small bits and fried them in my favorite heavy skillet over the hottest part of the fire. Often I will sauté the onions in butter to give them a lovely yellow color, most appealing to the eye, but this morning I used the rendered bacon fat from breakfast for an added richness. When the onions were soft and transparent, not quite beginning to caramelize, I poured in the eggs, stirring until they were set through. I then turned them onto my favorite blue crockery plate, which I'd had warming on the hearth.

I have made this dish many times, and each time I challenge myself to make it slightly different. In the past I have added sliced mushrooms with the onions or added a sharp cheese to the pan, letting it melt just slightly before serving. Today, I added snips of fresh parsley to brighten the flavor.

Hanoney

The detailed description of this simple omelette suggests that this dish was something that Halflings were quite fond of. This is probably due to it being easy to make, along with its extreme flexibility. Harald's notes included over twenty similar recipes, some of which were exact duplicates of this one, and most of them were titled "Another Hanoney".

3 eggs
1/2 medium onion, minced
2 Tbsp. butter
1 Tbsp. fresh parsley, chopped
salt and pepper to taste

Fry onions in butter until they start to caramelize. Beat eggs well, add parsley, and pour into pan with onions. Stir and cook until eggs set. Serve hot.

With fresh greens and herbs becoming available, I had a yen to add something with a light, spring taste to my repast. I gathered what I could from the wilder parts of the garden that were left to seed all winter, and those pots which I had brought into my small greenhouse to winter over – parsley, garlic, borage, mint and fennel, adding onions from my stores. When all were cleaned, I chopped them together in a bowl and laid on oil, vinegar and a little salt.

Salad of Spring Greens

[A simple chopped salad, the theme of ease and flexibility continues. A much oil-blotted sheet stuck in beside this, contained several variations on the simple vinaigrette dressing.]

1 cup spinach leaves
1/2 cup fresh parsley
1/2 cup fresh mint
1 fresh fennel, root and stalk
1/2 small onion, sliced
1 clove garlic, minced
Oil, vinegar, and salt to taste

Chop greens coarsely and place in a bowl. Add onions and garlic, and season with oil, vinegar, and salt.

I ate these together with a slab of toasted bread and soft new cheese, then finished with a wedge of the cherry tart I made the night before. Dotted with clotted cream, the pie went quite well with a mug of strong black tea.

To make the tart, I ground one pound of cherries in a mortar, a most time consuming task, but well worth in the end, and added thereto one pound of soft, mild cheese, sugar and eggs. It must be mixed well before adding the spices and rose petals, or the filling can look a bit lumpy. Put the mixture to a dish well lined with pastry, then cover with more pastry and bake until the crust be golden brown and the filling be full done.

[The description of the dish combined with other sources suggests the cheese used was something like ricotta or mascarpone]

Cherry Tart

1 pound dried cherries
1 pound ricotta cheese
1/2 cup sugar
3 eggs
1/2 tsp. ginger
1 tsp. cinnamon
1/8 cup rose petals
1 pinch black pepper

Pastry for double-crust pie

Grind cherries and mix with ricotta, sugar, and eggs. Add ginger, cinnamon, pepper, and rose petals. Mix well and pour into unbaked pie crust. Cover with top crust and bake at 350°F until top crust is golden brown.

After my repast, I sat on the bench outside my door, smoking a pipe to aid digestion and watching Merwyn turn the soil in the first of my vegetable patches. The lad had brought his own mid-morning repast – a round loaf of new bread, split down the center and filled with aged cheese, pickled cucumbers and cold bacon – though he did accept a wedge of the pie I offered. I have been trying to expand his culinary horizons beyond the simplest of fare, but have found this a very uphill battle. Merwyn is willing to grow anything I ask, he is rather less sanguine about eating it.

We worked side by side through the rest of the morning until well after midday. While physically demanding, the work of turning the soil, working in the rich compost did not much tax my brain. Thus, I found my thoughts turning often to my larder. Mentally, I toured the many pantries and the root cellars buried further back under the hill, pondering what I might make for luncheon and dinner.

In the early afternoon, I sent Merwyn home for his midday meal. Taking care to rinse the dirt from between my toes, I went into the cool dimness of the house and made my way to the kitchen. As much as was still to be done outside, I reasoned it best to start my supper to cook, as well as tending to my immediate hunger.

I went to my rearmost pantry, which stays much the coolest, to bring forth the fine shanks of lamb the butcher delivered this morning, to begin the slow hours of stewing it would need. While there, I saw the calf's tongue which I boiled last night, feeling it would answer well for midday dinner.

I first started my stew, hacking the shanks to small pieces, leaving the bones so the marrow might add their flavor and richness to the pot. I placed these in my deep iron pot with water and a fair quantity of dark ale – a tart cherry porter I have recently grown fond of – along with chopped onions and several handfuls of chopped herbs. Hanging the pot from the movable spit, I moved it to the sweet spot in the fire where the heat is most consistent.

I then turned my attentions to my current meal. I cut four thick slices from the tongue, which had been well boiled in broth, vinegar and wine and was thus firm but tender. I set a quantity of the boiling liquid in an earthen pot in the coals to warm while I fried the slices in a nice gobbet of butter until they were nicely browned and crusty. I laid the fried slices in the earthen pot to keep warm, then sliced mushrooms and fried them in the same pan with a dollop more butter, so as not to lose any of the crusty goodness.

I sat long at the table, enjoying my meal, while contemplating my afternoon's chores. Now and then I rose to stir the deep pot of stew and add the seasonings and other ingredients — first the roots which would benefit from the long cooking, and would serve, along with some grated bread to thicken the broth. I then went to my store of spices, common and dear, and added cinnamon and mace, along with cloves ground in the mortar. After another good stir, I covered the pot and pushed it back over the fire to simmer through the afternoon.

Greening Month, 20th day

The weather turned chill and blustery just after midday today, as often happens this time of year. While the turn is not unexpected, it does make working out of doors problematic, not to mention uncomfortable. Thus, I set Merwyn to work cleaning and honing the tools, whilst I set about making a hearty soup to take the cold from our bones – a favorite dish involving leeks.

White Leek Soup

2-3 leeks, cleaned and cut
1 onion, minced
6 chicken thighs, deboned
4 cups chicken broth
1/2 tsp. pepper
1/2 tsp. ginger
1/4 tsp. cinnamon
1/8 tsp. cloves
pinch saffron

Parboil and chop leeks and place in a pot with onion and broth. Bring to a boil, add chicken and spices, and simmer until chicken is cooked through. Serve hot.

The afternoon growing darker and thunder rattling the windows as the pot seethed on the hearth, I determined to raise Merwyn's spirits and my own with a dish of sweet cakes.

When first I made these sweet cakes from Heather's recipe, I sopped them in honey and clotted cream to serve, as she does at the Turnip. The next week, I baked them again, having just made a compote from the morning's newly picked berries and a sweet wine - one must pick berries early in the morning to have any harvest at all, otherwise the birds will have the greatest share. The combination was so harmonious; I must invite Heather over to sample it.

A Recipe for sweet cakes from Heather Drinkwater down at the Green Turnip: Take a good amount of good sugar and half again as much of the fairest flour, then add in fresh eggs to make a thin batter, and put in enough anise seeds and rosewater for it to be flavorful, then beat it very long that all is mixed together and it is soft, and put the batter in a shallow pan and put it in an oven to bake, and when it is cooked cut it in pieces, and if you keep the pieces in a sealed pot they will stay soft.

[Editor's Note: A second copy of this recipe, in a different and distinctly feminine hand, was folded and carefully tucked into the manuscript. The page on which it was written was frayed at one edge, as though it had been hastily torn from another book. The creases of the folds were no longer sharp, but soft and worn as though it had been opened and refolded many times. Either the recipe, or more likely it's donor, was much favored by the author.]

Sweet Cakes

In spite of the lack of leavening, these cakes turn out surprisingly soft and sponge-like, having a texture like a dense sort of angel food.

1 1/2 cup flour
1 cup sugar
4 eggs
2 Tbsp. anise seed
2 Tbsp. rose water

Put all ingredients together in a large bowl and beat well for 45 minutes (or mix for 3 minutes in a food processor). Pour batter into a greased baking pan and bake at 350°F until golden brown - about 15 minutes. Allow to cool for 5 minutes, then turn out of pan and slice.

Spent a good couple of hours visiting with Juniper and Oddy Greenfallow today. They have so many children running about that it makes my head spin, but Juniper's wonderful blackberry pie and Oddy's stash of pipe weed made it all worthwhile. On the way home I took a shortcut through their back pasture which they haven't used for years and learned their secret! There must be acres of land there that are entirely given over to berries. I think I saw several varieties, though not all were bearing fruit at this time of year. I gathered as many blackberries as I could fit into my hat and will have go back for more tomorrow. They'll make wonderful preserves for next winter.

Berry Compote

2 cups mixed berries
1 cup wine
1 cup water
1/3 cup sugar
1 tsp. cinnamon
1/2 tsp. ginger
1/4 tsp. salt

Put wine, water, sugar, and cinnamon into a pan and warm. Clean and wash berries, and add to wine. Add sandalwood, and salt and bring to a boil. Reduce heat and simmer until fruit is tender and compote thickens. Serve warm or cold.

Having sent Merwyn home early, the clouds and rain never lifting, I turned my thoughts toward supper. I craved the rich smell of roasting meats, with the tang of spice. A recent foray to the woods — a friend's excursion, not my own - had yielded fresh venison. While not as plump as an autumn deer, the meat was still quite flavorful. The leaner meat lends itself well to the long cooking method of a stew and benefits from the added liquid and tenderizing acidity of a strong red wine. Of course, if the deer is still too lean a dollop of good olive oil or fresh butter can help.

Venison Stew

1 lb. venison
2 cups wine
2 cups water
3 slices bread
1/2 medium onion, chopped
1/4 cup currants
1 tsp. salt
1/2 tsp. pepper
1/2 tsp. cinnamon
1/4 tsp. cloves
1/4 cup vinegar

Cut venison into small pieces and place in a pot with the wine and water. Bring to a boil, reduce heat, and simmer until venison is tender. Tear bread into pieces and place in a bowl. Add some of the broth from the pot and mix until bread turns to mush. Strain mixture back into pot, discarding the solids. Add remaining ingredients and cook until onions are tender and broth thickens. Serve hot.

"Milking month" (May)

Milking Month is the time to water the newly planted trees, to assure they are well established before the summer's heat Prune any unnecessary twigs, and graft those which need new buds. It is also time to amass great quantities of butter once the cows have freshened and to make strong cheeses.

~East Riding Horticultural Society Manual - Volume 1~

Milking month has come and the fields and meadows are in the full riotous bloom of spring flowers. The green carpets seem awash with the brilliant yellows of Daffodils, the reds and purples of tulips. I know I wax poetic, but it is hard not to do so when the weather is so fine. There is much work to do in the garden, pruning and watering, and I find myself working up more than my customary appetite.

Goodwife Carline Ateberry has kept me well supplied with new butter and freshly made cheeses. Some of these I will eat new, while others are put back in the deepest pantries, carefully wrapped, to age. I have brought forward one such round from last spring, now well matured – strong and sharp. I decided to make a tart with the cheese and some spring greens. The spicy sweetness of the pie pairs well with the flavor of a smoked ham. I fried a few thick slices in butter, and finished the meal with a plate of pickled vegetables made from the previous year's harvest.

I told that dolt to plant the mint in a tub, but did he listen? Now the mint is growing riotously throughout the lettuce and spinach. Some of it would be nice mixed with greens and cheese and made into tarts, but the rest will have to be hung up to dry. If it keeps its flavor well then I may be able to trade some of it, but I am doubtful. Once that plot is well harvested I shall have to set Merwyn to pull it all up by the roots and feed it to the pigs. That'll teach him to listen, and it should make the pig yard smell strange for a while.

Spring Tart

1/2 pound spinach, washed and chopped
1/2 cup chopped mint
2 eggs
1/2 cup grated parmesan
4 Tbsp. butter
1 Tbsp. sugar
2 Tbsp. currants
1/4 tsp. cinnamon
1/8 tsp. nutmeg

Mix all ingredients together. Put in single crust and bake at 350°F until done, about 45 minutes.

Woke to rain this morning, no thunder or lightning, just a steady downpour that looked fair to last the entire day. Since there was little I could do out of doors, I set Merwyn to transplanting herbs in the greenhouse and turned my own hand at reorganizing the root cellars and pantries. With last autumn's abundant harvest, I am still adequately stocked, though I look forward to the fresher tastes of summer. The stores, along with the brace of pigeons Merwyn snared, gave me thoughts on what would make a good luncheon. Stewed pigeon and boiled apples could cook through the morning with little tending and be ready when hunger drove us from our tasks.

Stewed Pigeons

With pigeon or squab sometimes harder to come by in modern groceries, you can use cut up chicken or Cornish game hens for this recipe. Chicken thighs stew well, are quite economical, and can approximate the gamier taste and texture of the pigeon.

3-4 pounds chicken
2 cups broth
1 clove garlic
1 Tbsp. parsley
1/2 tsp. marjoram
1/2 tsp. sage
1/4 tsp. pepper
1/4 tsp. ginger
1/8 tsp. cinnamon
1/2 tsp. salt
pinch cloves
pinch saffron

Cut chicken into large pieces. Place with remaining ingredients in a large pot and bring to a boil. Cover, reduce heat, and simmer until done - about 20 minutes.

Milking Month, 15th day

Merwyn brought one of his cousins with him today, one of the Bricklethorn brood from Woodmere. With the extra hands, we finished our work in the garden early, thus giving me more time to devote to cooking. As the butcher's lad had dropped off a brace of nice fat capons this morning, I resolved to roast one with a fine black sauce for dinner and stew the other for supper. New asparagus, just cut today, will make the perfect complement to both.

Black Sauce

1 capon liver
1/4 tsp. anise seed
1/4 tsp. grains of paradise, ground
1/4 tsp. ginger
1/4 tsp. cinnamon
1 Tbsp. bread crumbs
1/4 cup verjuice (sour grape juice)
2 Tbsp. butter

Cook livers and puree. Add spices, verjuice, butter or fat, and breadcrumbs. Bring to a boil, simmer, and serve hot.

If verjuice is not available, use 1 Tbsp. each of grape juice and lemon juice.

Today I was forced to admit that Merwyn was right. Last summer he wanted to plant the mint in half-barrels sunk into the ground, but I told him it was just a couple of plants, and besides, I like mint tea enough that I would use it faster than it could ever possibly grow. Now the beastly stuff is growing everywhere. We pull it up as thoroughly as we can, but still can't seem to kill it. I now have enough mint dried and put away to last me until death, and I am so weary of the taste of it. Maybe if I feed it to the goats it will improve the smell of their yard.

In addition to the mint running riot through the herb beds, the asparagus has gotten quite out of hand. At least the slender stalks are more immediately useful.

[Editor's Note: Due to the fragmentary nature of the text, it is impossible to know whether this entry or the contradictory one on page 16 was written first. However, given what we can deduce of Harald's general character, it is safe to assume that any revisionist history would skew in terms of his own cleverness.]

Boiled Asparagus

1 pound fresh asparagus
1/2 medium onion (about 1/2 cup chopped)
1/4 cup currants
2 Tbsp. butter, melted
1/2 tsp. ginger
1/4 tsp. cinnamon
1/8 tsp. cloves
1/8 tsp. nutmeg

Cut asparagus spears into pieces about 3 inches long, wash, and set aside. Put onions, and currants into a large pot of boiling water. Allow to cook until onions are tender. Add asparagus and cook until tender. Drain and add remaining ingredients. Serve hot.

I felt a bit unwell this morning, probably from the foul mist coming out of the fens to the west all night, and I was not up to making anything too fancy for first breakfast. Instead I plucked some fresh herbs from the olitory and cooked up some of the eggs I'd got the day before from Merrow Fuzzwort. A good helping of these eggs, with sauce and a glass of blackberry wine, fortified me enough to give Merwyn some pointers on cleaning up the grapevines. After that I felt up to the task of making a proper breakfast.

[Editor's Note: Though no particulars are listed regarding the sauce, depending on the herbs used, this dish would work with anything from a simple cream sauce to a Hollandaise, similar to Eggs Benedict]

Herbed Eggs

4 eggs
1/2 tsp. sage
1/4 tsp. nutmeg
1/4 tsp. pepper
1 Tbsp. butter

Crack eggs into a bowl, add spices, and beat well. Melt butter in a frying pan, pour in eggs, and cook over low heat until firm. Cut into long slices and serve hot.

Uncut, the eggs could be served over toasted bread or muffins, with a rich buttery sauce. Like many similar dishes, the seasonings can be adjusted depending on what is to hand. Also goes splendidly with roasted asparagus in cream sauce.

"Walking month" (June)

In Walking Month, time is spent in the larger fields - mowing meadows, harvesting barley and beating the wheat for planting. For the home gardener, when not helping his neighbors in the fields, it is time to prune the vines.

~East Riding Horticultural Society Manual - Volume 1~

This month has been living up to its name. I feel I have walked the village thrice around, going from neighbor's field to neighbor's field to lend a hand, and offer the benefit of my years of experience. I like to help where best I may, in and around my own garden's needs. The strenuous labor has left me with not only a lump on the head from the unwary swing of a scythe, but also a mighty appetite for the fresh greens and ripe fruits coming from my own modest field. I was all too willing to seek my own hearth when the Barrowclump brothers suggested I had perhaps helped them enough for the day, though I could see there was still much to do. I stopped only long enough to pick a handful of fresh carrots and some greens from their door patch on my way to my own kitchen.

The collards are finally big enough to start harvesting. For the past several weeks I've been watching them grow and remembering how old Granther used to cook them. I'm pretty sure he just boiled them with onions, spices, honey and vinegar. I'll give it a try this evening, but I suspect I'll have to give in and go visit cousin Gillyflower over in West Riding and see if she has the recipe. She'll expect me to bring some preserves with me, of course. I wonder if she'll believe me if I tell her I've run clean out. Of course, I can always take her some of the quince-rhubarb from last autumn. It did not come out quite to snuff, but she'll never taste the difference.

Buttered Greens

1 bunch collard greens
4 Tbsp. butter
1/2 medium onion, chopped
2 carrots, chopped
3 cloves garlic, minced
2 Tbsp. herbs de Provence
1 tsp. oregano
1 tsp. thyme
2 tsp. ginger
1 tsp. cumin
1/4 cup honey
1/2 cup balsamic vinegar
4 cups broth
4 cups water

Wash greens, chop them into large pieces, and set aside. In a large stockpot, sauté onion, carrots, and garlic until onions turn translucent. Add spices and the remaining ingredients, along with the greens. Bring to a boil, reduce heat, and simmer until greens are tender. Drain and serve over cubed bread.

The richness of the buttered greens giving me enough strength to carry on, I stuffed some small hens with eggs and sausage to roast. The birds can cook mostly untended, whilst I lay back in my favorite arm chair, a cold compress on my head and a mug of cider close to hand.

Stuffed Game Hens

4 game hens
1 lb. ground sausage
4 eggs, hard boiled
1 tsp. salt
1/2 tsp. pepper
1/8 cup currants
1/2 tsp. cinnamon
1/4 tsp. cloves
1/4 tsp. mace
1/4 tsp. ginger

Brown sausage in a frying pan, drain off fat, and set aside. Grate or finely chop eggs. Place in a bowl with sausage, spices, and currants and mix well. Stuff into game hens and bake at 350°F until hens and stuffing have an internal temperature of 165°F - about 2 hours.

Walking Month, 20th day
With the trees in the orchard and the berry brambles bearing fruit, I have spent many a day making pies. Any fruit will lend itself to a closed tart - cherry and berries early in the summer, apple and pear near its end. I always strive to balance the sweetness of the tree ripe fruit with some tartness or savory spice. For cherries, a hint of dried mustard with the cinnamon and ginger can enhance the flavor, while the denser flesh of pears, apples, and quince work well with acidity and the strong flavor of nutmeg, cardamom, or pepper. Of course, a slice of sharp yellow cheese, melted atop the crust of apple pie, adds a pleasant richness and bite.

(Fresh) Cherry Tart

2 lbs. fresh cherries, pitted
1 tsp. mustard
1/2 tsp cinnamon
1/4 tsp ginger
1 cup sweet wine
1 Tbsp. rose water
2 Tbsp. sugar

Pastry for single-crust pie

Mix cherries and spices, place into a tart shell, and bake at 350°F until cherries are tender. Put wine, rose water, and sugar into a small pan. Bring to a boil and simmer until bubbles begin to stack up. Pour over cherries and serve.

Toward the end of walking month, I found myself somewhat at a loss. Merwyn has taken himself off, to help his Bricklethorn cousins in the barley mow, he says. But he's given me no indication as to when he might come back and has taken my best hoe and trowel with him. Like as not, I'll never see those again, even when he does bother to return. Doing all the necessary work on my own, and without my favored tools, has left me quite wrung out and in need of strong sustenance to fill my belly and soothe my jangled nerves. Having set a nice fat capon to stew, I decided to make wine sops to go with it.

I first toasted slices from a hearty brown bread and spread them well with butter before lining a high sided plate. I sliced an orange and warmed the slices in the small pot with claret, though any other sweet red wine will work as well. Poured over the toasted bread, the wine gives a marvelous base for the cooked chicken. The sweet and spicy addition always raises my spirits.

Capon Soup

1 lb. chicken, cooked
4 slices bread, toasted
1 cup wine
1/2 cup sugar
1/2 tsp. cinnamon
1/4 tsp. ginger
1 Tbsp. butter
4 orange slices

Combine sugar and spices in a small saucepan and mix well. Add wine and stir until sugar is dissolved. Bring to a boil, reduce heat, add orange slices, and simmer until syrup begins to thicken. Place a toast slice in a dish and top with a serving of chicken. Pour enough syrup on top to soak toast. Serve hot.

I harvested the first of the new peas this morning, a task better suited to my defter hand than Merwyn's clumsy one, even if the dullard had bothered to return. He won't listen when I tell him to pluck each pod gently. He is more intent on getting the job done quickly than in doing it right. Of course, it took me most of the morning to pick and shell them, but I felt my patience made me deserving of a treat.

Of course, Merwyn does not appreciate the simple elegance of this summer dish. He says it looks like the peas didn't agree with someone's belly. Makes me just as happy he isn't here to share the pudding from the strawberries I harvested on my early morning constitutional.

Boiled Peas

1 cup peas
2 cups milk
1 egg
1 slice bread, ground
1/4 tsp. ginger
1 tsp. dried parsley
1/2 tsp. salt
saffron

Boil peas in water until tender and drain. Beat egg and milk well and add to peas, along with remaining ingredients. Bring to a low boil. Reduce heat, and simmer until thick. Serve hot.

I love lazy spring afternoons, when all the garden work is done and the bright sun shines down upon the leaves of the strawberry plants in the beds by the front door. Today there are hundreds of beautiful scarlet berries peeking out from under the leaves, each one calling out to be plucked before the birds and rabbits can spoil them. I think I'll have a small bowl full for a snack before dinner, maybe with some cream and a little honey, and then I'll use the rest to make a sweet stew for dessert after supper. The best part of it all, of course, is that Merwyn has gone home for the day and I am not expecting any company, so there will be no one with whom I must share these sweet beauties.

Strawberry Pudding

2 cups strawberries
1 cup red wine
1 cup milk
1/2 cup sugar
1/4 cup currants
1/2 tsp. ginger
1/2 tsp. cinnamon
1/8 tsp. pepper
pinch saffron
1 Tbsp. flour or corn starch

Clean and quarter strawberries. Simmer them in red wine until soft. Force berries and wine through a strainer to remove seeds and pulp. Add milk, currants, sugar, and spices, and return to low boil. Mix flour or corn starch with a little of the liquid, and then add back into the pot and stir until thick. Remove from heat and serve warm.

PART 2 - SUMMER

"Visiting month" (July)

In Visiting Month, the gardener should gather the apples and pears, taking care that the trees are not bearing overmuch fruit. Whenever there is a spare moment, begin to lay in the stores of wood to heat through the months of dark and cold.

~East Riding Horticultural Society Manual - Volume 2~

The month of mid-summer visiting is among my favorite times of the year. With so much produce available that is fresh and full of flavor, it is no trouble to arrive on a neighbor's doorstep with a tasty morsel and a few grains of gardening wisdom. If my neighbors prove not to be at home, as often occurs, I simply leave the covered dish and a note of friendly advice on their stoop. I think though I must start carrying a stub of pencil in my pocket, so that I might add a caution not to leave their fires burning or their windows ajar when they are from home.

Once I've made my rounds, I'll drop in the Green Turnip for a mug of ale and a few words with Heather, then return to my always carefully banked kitchen hearth. The tastiest morsels from the day's gathering, of course, I have kept safely at home.

Stuffed Carrots

8 very large carrots
1/ 2 lb. chicken liver
4 slices bread, ground
1 Tbsp. currants
1 Tbsp. chopped dates
1/8 tsp. cloves
1/8 tsp. mace
1/4 tsp. pepper
1 tsp. salt

Clean carrots, carve out the core, and set aside. Chop liver, add remaining ingredients, and mix well. Stuff filling into hollowed out carrots. Steam or bake carrots until filling is firm and reaches 165°F - about 40 minutes.

The pears from my trees seem small and hard this season, though I am certain I instructed Edelbert quite thoroughly on their care. I don't know how he does it but he seems to have immense skill at making all manner of growing things turn out small and sickly. The pears are no exception, with their fruits seeming to go from not quite ripe to overblown in a day. No matter. If I cannot eat them fresh from the trees, they will still cook up acceptably in a custard.

Pear custard tastes well when the pears are fresh from the trees. I also like to make this in winter with the pears I've tucked away. It reminds me of the warmth of summer when the rain and snow blusters about my chimney.

Pear Custard

4 pears
1 cup white wine
1/2 cup sugar
4 egg yolks
1 tsp. cinnamon
1/2 tsp. ginger

Peel and core the pears. Cut into small pieces and place in a saucepan along with white wine. Bring to a boil, and simmer until pears are soft - about 15 minutes. Allow to cool and then grind with mortar and pestle (or in food processor). Mix with remaining ingredients in a saucepan. Heat until it boils and becomes very thick - it will resemble oatmeal in texture. Serve warm or cold.

I got some lovely artichokes yesterday from Merrow Fuzzwort and boiled them up properly. Instead of eating them as I usually do, which is with lots of salted butter and cream, I set the bottoms aside to try a recipe that Merrow recommends enthusiastically. It was a difficult task on seeing the pieces all trimmed and cleaned to not eat them all, but I managed to keep a dozen or so. I then cooked them with spices, vinegar, and butter. Oh my, she was right! They're very tasty this way. I think next time though I'll start by buying three times as many artichokes as I can possibly eat, that way I can have my fill and still have enough to make this way for the next meal.

Artichokes

10 - 12 artichoke bottoms, cooked
1/2 tsp. pepper
1/2 tsp. cinnamon
1/2 tsp. ginger
2 Tbsp. water
1 Tbsp. large crystal sugar
4 Tbsp. butter
dash vinegar

Mix pepper, cinnamon, and ginger with water. Add artichoke bottoms, toss, and allow to marinate for 15 minutes. Place into baking dish and add butter and vinegar. Bake at 350° for 15 minutes. Sprinkle with sugar and serve.

This morning Merwyn brought a peck of spotted peas to me as part of a payment from Oddy Greenfallow for a piglet I'd sent to him last year. Thing is, I know the Greenfallows don't grow peas, so I have no idea where they actually came from. They looked quite fresh though, so I boiled them and then fried them up for lunch with some garlic and onion, and a bit of spice. I even shared some with Merwyn, which is probably fair as I think the piglet might have been his.

These peas would also make an excellent side dish for dinner or tea, or a fine main course for a late supper. If I want to make it heartier, especially when using dried peas in winter time, when they will take a long, low simmer to soften and cook through, I will boil the peas with the bone of a ham, or fry some cubes of belly fat with the onions.

Black-eyed Peas

2 cups black-eyed peas
1 medium onion, chopped
1 clove garlic
2 Tbsp. olive oil
1 tsp. salt
1/2 tsp. ginger
1/2 tsp. cinnamon
1/8 tsp. cloves
1/8 tsp. nutmeg

Boil peas in water until tender, drain and set aside. Fry onions in olive oil until they start to turn translucent. Add remaining ingredients and fry until everything is cooked through and hot.

Another excellent summer supper! Heather Drinkwater suggested a simple soup made of peas in broth to use up some of my bumper crop. I'll make it this evening. The remaining rosemary bread from lunch should go well with the herbs in the soup. It can cook while I make my last rounds through the garden of an evening to make certain Edelbert has done all the tasks I set him for the afternoon. I hadn't thought anyone could need more supervision than Merwyn, but it seems I was mistaken.

Green Peas

2 cups peas
4 cups beef broth
2 Tbsp. parsley
2 tsp. sage
1 tsp. savory
salt to taste

Place all ingredients in a large pot and bring to a boil. Simmer until peas are tender, about 20 minutes.

Coming back from an amble with Oddy Greenfallow, I caught a brace of coneys making a feast in the lettuce beds, the chewed tops of my prize parsnips scattered about them. So brazen were they, the fiends didn't even budge when I walked through the gate, only staring at me with their beady eyes, ears twitching. A few swift stones later, their thieving days were done. Now they'll be a feast for me.

Coney in Gravy

4 lbs. rabbit
1 medium onion, chopped
2 Tbsp. olive oil
1 cup red wine
2 cups chicken broth
1/2 tsp. black pepper
1/2 tsp. mace
1/4 tsp. ginger
1/4 tsp. cloves
1/4 tsp. cinnamon
1/4 cup red wine vinegar
salt 1/4 tsp.
1 cup bread crumbs (2 slices)

Sear pieces of meat briefly in a large pot and set aside, using olive oil as necessary. Sauté onions in remaining oil until tender. Return the meat to the pot and add wine, broth, mace, cloves, pepper, and cinnamon. Bring to a boil and simmer for one hour. Add bread crumbs, ginger, vinegar, and salt just before serving.

In years past I have attempted to craft wines from my own harvest. My efforts have yielded indifferent and uneven success, usually producing more vinegar than drinkable vintages. To save myself unpleasantness, I have since determined either to purchase or barter for my cellar. This cherry wine was a particularly good year from Robyn Gracebottle's vineyard at Riverside. Since I bought nearly his entire production last year and promised to do likewise in the future, I was able to wheedle the recipe out of him.

Cherry Wine

4 lbs. fresh cherries
1 1/2 lbs. sugar
1/2 gallon water
1 cup strong tea
2 tsp. wine yeast

Wash cherries and remove the stems. Place them in a large kettle and crush them well. Cover and allow to stand overnight. Strain out solids using a sieve or linen cloth. Add water and sugar, and bring to a boil. Allow to cool, add remaining ingredients, and pour into fermentation vessel. Rack into a clean fermenter after two weeks, again in two months, and one last time two months after that. Rack into clean bottles and store in a cool, dark place.

"Weed Month" (August)

The deepest summer's heat brings also the greatest proliferation of weeds. The gardener must be vigilant to attend his plants. Then too, he must look ahead to the work of the busy harvest to come.

~East Riding Horticultural Society Manual - Volume 2~

A week of scant rain and warmer temperatures have left the beds and rows of my garden looking a bit droopy. Merwyn has spent the morning hauling buckets and watering cans from the pump in the yard. It is heavy work, and as I look out the kitchen window, I can see the sheen of sweat on his brow. As a reward for his toil, I have elected to make one of his favorite dishes for luncheon. The slightly sweet and spicy creamed sauce on the chicken pairs well with a fresh green salad and conserved cherries in summer, but it is good and filling at any time of year.

Started a batch of creamed chicken early this morning so it would be ready for lunchtime. It's best if it simmers for at least a couple of hours. You can't rush a good thing, but I usually try to anyways!

While a crock of this dish is generally sufficiently filling, I have also served it in bowls made from hollowed day old loaves of brown bread. Others have suggested pouring the mixture over rice, but that would see to me too much of a good thing.

Creamed Chicken

1 pound chicken
2 cups milk
2 egg yolks
2 Tbsp. rice flour
1 Tbsp. sugar
1/4 tsp. galingale
1/4 tsp. salt
1/8 tsp. cinnamon
1/8 tsp. cloves
1/8 tsp. mace

Chop the chicken finely and place in a large pot. Whisk together almond milk egg yolks and rice flour, and add to chicken. Add spices and bring to a low boil. Simmer until thick, and serve hot.

The cherries were abundant this month, so bountiful in fact that I knew even with Merwyn's enthusiastic help, I could not eat them all before they began to go off. As this would have been a great pity, I set to conserving them. Whilst I ate a bowl of the fresh fruit with clotted cream, I placed a good two pounds of the ripe cherries, pitted and picked over, into an iron kettle. After adding a pound of fine white sugar for each equal measure of fruit, I swung the pot over that part of the fire which burns with a low and steady flame and glowing coals – the type of fire my Da used to call 'soft'. The smell of the gently simmering mixture turned my mind happily to all the things I could make with the conserve once it was done. When the level in the pot had reduced by a third, I removed it from the heat, added rose water and the spices and set it to cool. Once fully cooled, the sweet and shiny result can be eaten immediately on toasted oat cakes or custard, or stored in pots well sealed with wax.

[Editor's note: conserves that will be used quickly can be kept in a refrigerator. For long term storage, canning in sterilized jars is recommended.]

Conserved Cherries

2 lbs. cherries, pitted
2 lbs. sugar
1/4 cup water
2 Tbsp. rose water
1/2 tsp. cinnamon
1/4 tsp. cloves

Place cherries, water, and sugar into a large pot and bring to a boil. Reduce heat and simmer, stirring occasionally and mashing some of the cherries with a spoon. When mixture reaches 220°F remove from heat and store in refrigerator.

[Editor's Note: The page with this recipe was tucked into the manuscript, carefully folded, with the following note in Harald's hand scribbled on the outside.]

White mead recipe from old Fortenberry. Never had much luck with fermentation. Have my doubts about all the flowers. He promised to bring over a bottle from last year's batch to change my mind.

White Metheglin

3 lbs. honey
3 quarts water
1 egg
1 Tbsp. strawberry leaves
1/2 Tbsp. violet leaves
1/4 Tbsp. sorrel
1 Tbsp. rosemary leaves
1 Tbsp. thyme leaves
3 sage leaves
6 cloves
1/4 tsp. nutmeg
1/2 tsp. ginger
1 package wine yeast

Mix the honey, water, and egg in a large, non-reactive pot. Bring to a boil and simmer, skimming off any scum that forms on the surface. Add herbs, remove from heat, and allow to cool. Add cloves, nutmeg, ginger, and yeast and transfer to a fermenting container. Allow to ferment and rack when fermentation slows. Rack again after 3 and 6 months, and bottle after one year. Store 6 months before drinking.

Another bushel of peas harvested. The peas seem to have exploded this season, overgrowing their bed and spreading almost as extensively as the mint. There are so many of them, I have had to comb through Ma's old books of receipts to come up with more things to do with them. I think they should be especially good cooked with eggs and butter in a pie, perhaps with a little sour apple juice poured on top. Of course most of the crop has been put out under screens to dry in the sun. I'm sure I'll appreciate them in the lean time, but they're so much nicer when fresh.

Tart of Peas

3 cups peas
2 eggs
2 Tbsp. butter, melted
1/2 tsp. salt
1/4 tsp. pepper
1/8 cup verjuice

Pastry for double-crust pie

Boil peas, drain, and mash. Add eggs, butter and spices and pour into bottom crust. Cover with top crust, cutting a small hole at the top. Bake at 350°F for 30 minutes. Remove from oven, pour verjuice in the hole, return to the oven, and bake for an additional 30 minutes.

If verjuice is not available, use 1 Tbsp. each of grape juice and lemon juice.

I got a large sack of mustard seed from the Barrowclump brothers last week and finally got around to putting it up today. Their back field has turned out a fine crop of the stuff for two years now and it seems they've got plenty to spare. The seeds are lovely even and round, and the little blighters are hard too. Grinding them took so much out of me that I had to rest with a large glass of cherry wine until my strength came back. The job is done now, and the mustard is properly vinegared and aging in a crock in the third root cellar. By the time I'm down to dried sausage or salt ham this winter it will be in fine shape, though now that I'm thinking about it I'm not sure I'll be able to wait that long.

Oddy Greenfallow says he doesn't understand why I bother making my own mustard, when Goodwife Carline Ateberry makes it by the tub and is willing to barter it for jam and turnips. But I have always found hers too sour and I think she uses an inferior vintage. I put care into my hams and roasts. Why would I use anything but the best to dress them?

Mustard

1/4 cup mustard seeds
1/4 cup vinegar
1/4 cup white wine
1 tsp. honey
1 tsp. ginger
1/2 teaspoon salt

Place all ingredients into a glass bowl, cover, and allow to rest for 2 to 3 days. Grind with a mortar and pestle or food processor to desired consistency. Will keep in the refrigerator for up to 6 months.

"Harvest month" (September)

The zenith of a gardener's year. Now is the time to bring in the vegetables and fruits, nuts and grains, and enjoy the bountiful table of all he has labored to bring forth. Be sure to collect the seed to lay aside for planting in the spring.

~East Riding Horticultural Society Manual - Volume 2~

It looks like the apples from the winter quitten tree are finally ripe! They're such small little things, but their so wonderfully aromatic. I've already had second breakfast but I know Merwyn won't mind if I take a few and duck back into the kitchen for a bit while he finishes up picking them. I've still got some fresh eggs and I just can't resist the two fried up together with butter and spices. I suppose I should make sure to save some for Merwyn as well, though it will be very difficult.

Eggs & Apples

1 apple
2 to 3 eggs
1 Tbsp. butter
1/8 tsp. ginger
pinch cinnamon
pinch cloves
pinch pepper
pinch saffron, ground

Peel, core, and slice apples, and Parboil them in water until just tender. Drain off the water and then fry them in butter. Remove from pan and set aside. Beat eggs and fry, adding apples back to the pan just before they're finished. Sprinkle with fine spice powder and saffron. Serve hot.

This year the peach tree put out only a small crop. I don't know how many more productive years it has left in it, so I'll have to graft a couple of saplings to make sure I have enough to keep me in pies. It occurred to me that the thing must be at least a dozen years old. To think that for the past twelve years I haven't had to beg the Greenfallows for any of their fine fruit. Strange that they never figured out who it was that took cuttings from their prize tree. Still, I must have pies, especially when made with some of Gracebottel's finest red baked in!

Peach Tart

5-6 peaches
1/4 cup red wine
3/4 cup sugar
1/2 tsp. cinnamon
1/2 tsp. ginger
1/4 tsp. salt

Pastry for double-crust pie

Peel peaches, remove pits, and slice. Parboil in water until just tender. Drain well and place in pie crust. Make syrup of sugar, spices, and wine. Pour over peaches and cover with top crust, making a few slits in the top. Bake at 425°F for 10 minutes, then reduce heat to 350°F and bake until done, about 30-40 minutes more.

I got some fresh lamb from Oddy Greenfallow this afternoon in trade for some apples. They always have too many males in the flock at the end of summer, so he's willing to practically give it away. I put it to cook in a pot over the coals with some onions and parsnips from the garden and the smell has completely distracted me from working for the rest of the day. I was going to have it with some bread for supper but I had a little taste just a bit ago and I think it's tender enough, so I think it will be now instead. I'll have to find something else to eat later.

Lamb Stew

1 - 2 lb. lamb
2 parsnips, peeled, cored, and chopped
1 medium onion, chopped
2 Tbsp. olive oil
1 cup red wine
1/2 tsp. salt
1/2 tsp. cinnamon
1/4 tsp. ginger

Cut lamb into bite-sized pieces. Fry onions with olive oil in a large pot until tender. Add lamb and cook until pieces are browned on all sides. Add remaining ingredients along with enough water to cover, bring to a boil, and simmer until done - about 1 hour.

When I told Merwyn that I was going to make Da's favorite chicken dinner, the one stuffed with fruit and herbs, he looked at me like I was quite mad. "Only a nutter stuffs fruit in a chicken," he said to me. Of all the gall, calling my Da a nutter! I sent him on his way back home and told him not to come back. I simply will not have someone with such plebian tastes working in my garden!

Chicken Stuffed with Fruit

1 roasting chicken, approx 4 lbs.
1 pear
1 apple
1 cup grapes
1 Tbsp. parsley
1 tsp. sage
1/2 tsp. savory
1 clove garlic
2 Tbsp. pan drippings from the chicken
2 Tbsp. wine
1/2 tsp. salt
1/2 tsp. ginger
1/8 tsp. cinnamon
pinch cloves
pinch nutmeg

Peel, core, and chop the apple and pear into quarter inch pieces. Place fruit, herbs, and spices into a large bowl and mix well. Stuff into the chicken, place in a roasting pan, cover, and roast at 350°F until meat reaches 165°F - about 2 hours.

Remove fruit from chicken and place in a saucepan over medium heat. Add drippings from chicken, wine, and spices. Cook until heated through. Serve hot along with meat.

Small birds remain plentiful this time of year, and are a never ending irritant to a gardener trying to bring in his harvest. Edmer, Merwyn's Bricklethorn cousin who is working for me now, brought in several small sparrows he had snared in the blackberries. They had been well fed from my brambles, so now they'll feed us well in pies.

Sparrow Pies

Sparrows aren't commonly eaten in modern society, but a reasonable approximation can be found using small pieces of dark meat chicken.

1 - 2 lbs. chicken thighs, deboned
1/4 cup grated parmesan
2 Tbsp. butter, melted
1 tsp. sugar
1/4 tsp. ginger
1/4 tsp. salt

Pastry for double-crust pie

Mix ingredients together, place in pie crust and cover with top crust. Bake at 350°F until filling reaches 165°F - about 1 hour.

The richness of the pies called for something sharp as a complement. Turning to the basket of vegetables just brought in and washed, I chose to make a quick salad of cucumber and radishes. Take cucumber and slice them down, peel and all, about the thickness of a copper coin, then quarter. Trim a handful of radishes and slice the same, so there be about half as much as the cucumbers. Mix good oil and vinegar with a touch of salt and pepper and a sprinkling of fresh snipped dill. Toss the dressing over the vegetables. It is good if eaten right away, but better if let to sit an hour or more.

Cucumber Salad

1 large or 2 small cucumbers
5 radishes
1 Tbsp. olive oil
1 Tbsp. apple cider vinegar
1/2 tsp. dill
salt and pepper to taste

Clean vegetables, cut into thin slices and place in serving bowl. In a separate bowl, combine vinegar, olive oil, and spices, whisking until mixed. Toss with the vegetables and allow to rest an hour before serving.

PART 3 - AUTUMN

"Hunting month" (October)

Now that the harvest is mainly passed, and hunters turn to the fields to lay in game for the cold season, the gardener must turn his mind to preserving what he has grown. There will be wine to make, honey and beeswax to store. He should also bring indoors those trees and plants which will not survive the coming cold.

~East Riding Horticultural Society Manual - Volume 3~

Hunting month is upon us. While I look forward to the autumn fattened deer, I am not much for the chase. Let others, younger and more spry, tear through the forest after game. I am for my pipe, the stuffed chair at my hearth, and the contemplation of the stores I have laid in. I have claim to a fair share of venison, though, in barter with a friend who's a taste for my pickles and preserves.

I had the luck to get a hold of several deer kidneys today! I'm not sure where Edmer got them and I'm not going to ask. It's been so long since I had kidney pie that I was afraid I'd forgotten how to make it, but my careful notes came to the rescue. There, underneath Merrow's instructions for making lemon tarts was Ma's old recipe, and with the smell of the kidneys boiling it all came back to me.

Humbles of a Deer

1 lb. deer kidneys
1/2 cup dates, pitted and chopped
1/2 cup currants
1 Tbsp. sugar
1 tsp. cinnamon
1/2 tsp. ginger
1/8 tsp. cloves
1/8 tsp. mace
2 Tbsp. butter
4 Tbsp. butter
1 Tbsp. sugar
1/2 tsp. cinnamon
1/4 tsp. ginger

Pastry for double-crust pie

Slice the kidneys and boil them well in water until they are cooked through. Allow them to cool, and then mince them. Place them into a bowl, along with the dates, currants, sugar, and spices. Mix well and put into a 9-inch pie crust. Top with pats of butter and cover with top crust. Make a half-inch hole in the center of the pie. Bake at 350°F until the crust is golden brown.

Melt the butter in a small saucepan. Mix sugar, cinnamon, and ginger together and add to butter. Bring to a boil and then pour as much as possible into the hole in the top of the pie. Serve warm.

Merrow Fuzzwort brought me some positively beautiful Damson plums today. I'm not sure where she got them though, as both of her plum trees got the blight two years back and didn't leaf this spring. Perhaps I should have Merwyn, or rather Edmer, get a sapling from the society and plant it by the wall near the front garden. The other trees there are doing well enough, and I do like plums quite a bit. I think that I shall cook these in some sweet red wine and make them into a tart for a late-night snack. With luck there will be a bit left over for breakfast.

Plum Tart

8 medium plums
2 cups red wine
1/2 cup sugar
1/2 tsp. cinnamon
1/4 tsp. ginger

Pre-baked tart crust

Peel plums and remove the pits. Mix spices with sugar and place in a large saucepan with wine. Bring to a boil and add plums. When the mixture returns to a boil, reduce heat and simmer until plums are tender, about 10 minutes. Remove plums from syrup with a slotted spoon and set aside in a bowl. Boil the remaining liquid until reduced to about 1/3 cup. Remove from heat. Place plums into tart crust, cover with syrup, and allow to cool.

Edmer had good luck hunting yesterday and managed to kill a young boar. He and his family roasted it and ate what they could, but of course there is still plenty to go around, so he brought a large portion with him this morning. I cut it up, wrapped it in pastry with some butter and spices, and baked it for lunch. I thought it turned out quite well, but I couldn't tell if he thought so. Edmer isn't really the talkative sort. I don't think I've ever heard him use a word of more than one syllable. In fact, now that I think about it, I'm not sure I've ever heard him talk at all.

Baked Boar Pie

2 lbs. boar or pork
1/2 tsp. cloves
1/4 tsp. mace
2 tsp. pepper
1/2 tsp. sage
2 Tbsp. sugar
4 Tbsp. butter

Crust for double-crust pie

Boil or slow-cook the pork until tender. Allow to cool and then chop into small pieces. Add spices and sugar, put into pie crust, dot with butter, cover with a top crust, and bake at 350°F until golden brown - about 30 minutes. Serve hot.

Lunch today was a stew made from leeks and carrots from the side garden beds. I remember auntie Wallflower making some kind of milk and leek soup, but she was a stingy one with the recipes so I had to trust my instincts. It didn't quite turn out like she used to make, though I suspect that's because I didn't accidentally dump pipe ash into the pot as she would often do. I expect my version tastes a good bit better without.

Leek Potage

2 lbs. leeks
1/2 lb. carrots, diced
4 slices bacon, chopped
3 cups milk
1/4 cup flour
1/4 tsp. cinnamon
1/4 tsp. salt

Trim and wash leeks, keeping only the white parts. Chop them well and boil along with carrots in water until tender. Drain, discarding the liquid, and place in a pot with the bacon. Sauté until bacon is thoroughly cooked. Add flour and spices, and mix well. Slowly stir in milk and bring to a low boil. Simmer until thick.

Hunting Month, 25th day
Went to the kitchen for a bit of a snack and saw a peck of nice, tart
apples sitting on the table. Nothing to do but cook some up sweet with
milk and rosewater. It really did help sooth my nerves after such a
harrowing day helping Edmer with the beehives. Every time one of the
little fellows would light upon him he would shriek and go off on a run.
I could have continued on by myself but half of the time he still had the
hive with him. I really think he would spend hours trying to stick his
elbow in his own ear if I suggested to him that it was possible.

Cooked Apples

4 apples
3 cups water
2 cups milk
1/4 cup honey
1/4 tsp. salt
2 tsp. rosewater (optional)

Peel, core, and slice apples. Bring water to a boil and add apple
slices. Cook until soft and then strain, discarding liquid. Chop
apples into small pieces and place in a pot with remaining
ingredients. Bring to a low boil, reduce heat, and simmer until
thick. Serve hot.

Whilst I understand the process for making cider, and could possibly if it were required, make a passable brew, I find the whole enterprise far too taxing. As with the Gracebottel Vineyard for my wines, I am fortunate that the next village over possesses one of the finest cider presses within twenty leagues. Better yet, Master Tancred is an expert at coaxing just the right balance of crisp sweetness from the apples. For a part of my orchard's yield of both apples and pears, he keeps me amply supplied throughout the year.

Hard Cider

1 gallon apple cider
1/4 tsp. wine yeast

Place cider in a fermenting bottle and add yeast. Seal the bottle with a fermentation lock. The cider should start to ferment within 48 hours and slow down around 5 days later. Once bubbling has nearly stopped, carefully transfer (rack) the cider to a clean bottle, leaving the sediment behind. Seal the second bottle with a fermentation lock and allow to ferment for another three weeks. Rack again into a clean bottle. Cider is then ready to drink, but the flavor will improve if it is allowed to age for a couple of months.

Note that the cider used should not contain any preservatives, or it may not ferment.

"Blood month"   (November)

Once the frost begins to paint the ground, the gardener should gather the last fruits of the earth – acorns to feed the pigs, chestnuts – and store them well. Pull root vegetables from the earth and move them to a root cellar to guard them from frost and decay.

~East Riding Horticultural Society Manual - Volume 3~

Yesterday for dinner I cooked rather a lot more pork than I intended, so I had a lot left overs today that really should be eaten quickly. Rather than just have it plain, I made up a large pie with cheese and eggs and spices and cooked the stuff a second time. It was really quite good, if I say so myself. I had some for lunches and again at dinner and now I have none left for supper. I may have to ask Merwyn tomorrow if he will pop on back home and fetch some more pork. His family raises the best pigs, and I'm sure half of what they're fed is the leavings from my gardens. The pigs that is, not Merwyn's family.

Rich Pork Pie

2 - 3 lbs. cooked pork
4 eggs
1 cup mozzarella, grated
1/2 tsp. pepper
1/2 tsp. ginger
1/4 tsp. cinnamon
1/8 tsp. cloves
1/4 cup pine nuts
1/4 tsp. salt
pinch saffron

Pastry for a double-crust pie

Cut pork into approximately 1 inch pieces. Combine with eggs, cheese, pine nuts and spices in a large bowl. Mix well and place into bottom crust. Cover with top crust and bake at 350° until golden brown - about 30 minutes. Serve either hot or cold.

Blood Month, 7th day
A cool, autumn night is the perfect time for a large bowl of beef stew and
some dense, crusty bread. I only got the beef late this afternoon so I
didn't have time to let it cook for as long as I usually like, so I made
sure to cut it into small enough pieces. I used plenty of onions to help the
meat get tender, and added cinnamon of course. Ma always said beef
stew just wasn't right without cinnamon.

Beef Stew

1 1/2 lbs. beef
1/2 tsp. cinnamon
1/4 tsp. cloves
1/4 tsp. mace
1/2 tsp. pepper
1 medium onion, minced
1 Tbsp. parsley
1/2 tsp. sage
water

3 slices bread
1/4 cup vinegar
pinch saffron
1/2 tsp. salt

Cut beef into 1/2 inch cubes. Place in a large pot with enough
water to cover and bring to a boil. Simmer for about 20 minutes
and strain, reserving liquid (this is only to help remove any scum
that forms on the surface during boiling). Put beef and broth back
into pot, and add onions and spices. Return to a boil and cook until
meat is tender. Meanwhile, tear up bread slices and place in a bowl
with the vinegar and enough broth to completely moisten it. When
the beef is cooked, strain the bread mixture through a fine strainer
into the pot, discarding the bread solids. Add saffron and salt and
simmer until the soup thickens slightly. Serve hot.

I went out to check the gardens this morning and found that the coleflowers are all filled out and ready for harvest. I really can't abide coleflowers but they grow so very well and Merrow Fuzzwort is always so happy to take them in trade. I just don't understand why though. The only way they're edible is if you boil them with onions and currants, and then meddle them up with some butter and cheese. Yes, that's the only proper way to eat the things. I expect I'll have to cook up a batch for supper tonight to be sure they're as bad as I remember, or maybe for lunch.

Cauliflower

1 head cauliflower
1/2 medium onion (about 1/2 cup chopped)
1/2 tsp. thyme
1/2 cup grated soft cheese
1/4 cup currants
2 Tbsp. butter, melted
1/2 tsp. salt

Cut cauliflower into pieces, wash, and set aside. Put onions, and currants into a large pot of boiling water. Allow to cook until onions are tender. Add cauliflower and cook until tender. Drain, finely chop or grind, add remaining ingredients, and mix well. Serve hot.

When venison is hewn small and roasted with bacon and wine, the effect is most delicious. I rounded out the meal with a wheat porridge which can be served either sweet or savory, then filled in the corners with those few sweet cakes which Merwyn and I had not eaten at luncheon. Merwyn often says he'd rather have venison than mutton, but I think that's because his brother does the hunting so he gets the venison for free. I also prefer venison, but that's because the taste of mutton always makes me think of wet mittens.

Roasted Venison

2 lbs. venison steaks
4 strips bacon
2 cups red wine
1 cup water
1 tsp. cinnamon
1 tsp. ginger

Cut venison and bacon into small pieces. Place into roasting pan with remaining ingredients. Cover and bake at 350°F until tender - about 1 hour. Serve hot with wheat porridge.

I was sitting by the fire and reading, as I am wont to do on such chilly nights, when it occurred to me that I was still a bit peckish from second supper. There were a couple of eggs left in the pantry, and flour of course, so I thought I might make up some biscuits. Then I remembered the rest of the porridge that was still in the kettle. No sense in letting that go to waste now. Mother always said that porridge was best eaten just before bed, and who am I to question her? I added a chopped up apple, a little cream, some honey, and a smidge of cinnamon, just like she used to do, and then I warmed it all by the fire.

Wheat Porridge

This savory porridge is good on its own, sprinkled with sugar and cinnamon it makes an excellent breakfast. It also serves well as a base for the roasted venison. The pan drippings from the roasted meats soak in, giving the dish a satisfying richness, as though it will stick with you through the long nights of winter to come.

1 cup cracked wheat
2 cups water
2/3 cup milk
2 egg yolks
1/2 tsp. salt
pinch saffron

Bring water to a boil and add wheat. Return to a full boil, reduce heat, cover, and simmer for about 15 minutes or until water water is absorbed and wheat is tender. In a separate bowl mix egg yolks and milk. Add to wheat along with remaining ingredients and stir well. Serve hot - sprinkle with sugar and/or cinnamon if desired.

"Dark month" (December)

Though the gardener may wish to hibernate like the smaller beasts during the dark and cold at the nadir of the year, he must resist this temptation, at least in part. As the rains fall, he must check his beds and fields for standing water, and drain them as needed. If he must stay indoors, then he can turn his hand to enjoying the fruits of his summer's labors.

~East Riding Horticultural Society Manual - Volume 3~

I spent a productive morning sitting on the porch with a slingshot, and knocked down several of those fat doves. It was a bit nippy out, and I think the cold air was making their little bird brains a bit sluggish as they pecked at the bread crumbs I had scattered by the front step. Now that I have a nice bunch of doves I think I'll reward myself by making them into an easy stew for lunch. They should cook up nicely with a bit of wine and some bacon, and then I'll serve them with toast and maybe have a glass of cider or two.

Small Birds in Gravy

1 lb. chicken thighs
1/2 cup red wine
1 cup water
1/4 cup cooked bacon pieces
1/2 tsp. salt
1/4 tsp. pepper
1/4 tsp. ginger

Place all ingredients in a large pot. Bring to a boil, reduce heat, cover, and simmer until meat is tender - about 40 minutes.

Bought a nice gammon of bacon from that wretched little toad down towards West Riding. He overcharged me again. Next fall I'll have to remember to send Merwyn on a nighttime visit to his apple orchard to collect the balance due. At any rate, the bacon is just the right size for my favorite baking pan, so I think I'll wrap it up in dough, along with spices and some hard eggs. Then I can bake it for dinner and maybe have some left for breakfast tomorrow.

Baked Bacon

2 lb. unsliced bacon, cut in large pieces
2 Tbsp. parsley, chopped
2 Tbsp. sage, chopped
6 eggs, hard boiled
1/4 tsp. cloves
1/4 tsp. mace
1/2 tsp. pepper
2 Tbsp. butter, melted

pastry for double crust pie

Finely chop eggs and place in a large bowl with pieces. Add herbs, spices, and butter and mix everything together well. Place mixture into bottom crust, cover with top, and bake at 350°F degrees until golden - about 45 minutes.

Dark Month, 12th day

We're going to have a bumper crop of onions this year. Merwyn thinned out the rows and left me with a large basked of the prettiest little onions. Da always said that onions go with everything, and there is something to that, I suppose. There is very little you can't make with onions, except maybe a lemon pie. You can bake them, fry them, put them in stew. Of course there were days when Ma wouldn't let Da back in the house until he'd washed out his mouth, but Da didn't mind a bit. He'd just say, "That's what ale is for, Harald." At any rate, I know precisely what to do with these little beauties. They're going to be cooked up in a nice milk sauce, green from cumin. That'll be the perfect side dish for the baked bacon.

Onions with Cumin Sauce

1 pound (3 cups) pearl onions, peeled
2 cups milk
2 slices bread
1/2 tsp. cumin
1/4 tsp. salt

Soak bread in milk until it falls apart, and then strain, discarding the solids. Place liquid along with remaining ingredients in a saucepan and bring to a boil. Reduce heat and simmer until onions are tender, stirring frequently to prevent burning.

I dropped off some pork at the baker's and that fat and lazy good-for-nothing tried to tell me it wasn't enough to make up for all the cakes I'd eaten since the start of the year. It's not my fault that he makes those things so short that they crumble away to nothing on my pantry shelves. We argued a bit and he finally relented and let me go home with a couple of loaves of the most wonderfully dense bread. Beneath a crust that a crow couldn't break through is a crumb that is amazingly pale and soft. One of the loaves is going to be for lunch, but the other is destined for some bread pudding tonight. Now I must remember to take a few jars of quince preserves over to the baker's sometime in the next Tillingmonth.

Bread Pudding

1/2 pound bread
1/2 pound raisins
1/3 cup sugar
2 cups milk
1/2 cup butter, melted
2 Tbsp. rose water
3/4 tsp. nutmeg
4 eggs

Remove the crusts from the bread. Cut it into one-inch cubes. Mix sugar with raisins and combine with bread cubes, making sure the raisins are distributed evenly. Place bread mixture in a casserole dish. In a separate bowl, mix butter, milk, eggs, nutmeg and rosewater. Pour carefully over bread cubes. Garnish with sliced dates. Cover and bake in 325° oven for 45 minutes or until a knife put into the center comes out clean. Sprinkle with a coarse-grained sugar and bake uncovered for 15 more minutes. Serve hot.

I had a craving this evening for something sweet but none of the preserves in the pantry quite appealed to me, so I thought I'd try my hand at making a treat that Willow Gracebottel suggested the last time I was visiting. It involved taking equal amounts of wine and honey and cooking it up with ginger and spices until it is thick. She said to dip it with cakes, but I found it quite fine poured over yesterday's bread pudding. When that was gone I had the rest of the syrup spread thickly on toasted bread.

Wine Syrup

1/4 cup wine
1/4 cup honey
1/8 tsp. ground ginger
pinch salt
pinch pepper
fresh ginger

Peel fresh ginger and chop very finely. Set aside.

Put wine, honey, ground ginger, salt, and pepper into a saucepan and bring to a boil. Reduce to medium heat and simmer until bubbles start to stack - or until syrup is thick when cool. Spoon over bread pudding or toast and sprinkle with a little fresh ginger. Serve hot.

PART 4 - WINTER

"Smoking month" (January)

At the beginning of the winter season, the gardener will find himself, like his garden, mostly fallow. As Smoking Month progresses, and the days slowly begin to lengthen, his work will turn to maintenance – sharpening tools, and whittling stakes to support tender new vines – all tasks that can be done with a pipe by the hearth.

If the gardener has a hothouse or conservatory to hand, he may start the early seeds, though they will need much tending even indoors. If not, he will need to tend only his compost and manure piles for the spring and summer to come.

~East Riding Horticultural Society Manual - Volume 4~

Roasted a capon for dinner tonight. I cooked the thing the way great-uncle Broadknuckle liked, with herbs and eggs for the stuffing. Ma always said that fruits were the proper way to stuff a capon, but Broadknuckle didn't care much for fruits. He said they disagreed with him something fierce. "Eggs!" he would say. "Eggs come out of birds, right? Eggs should go into birds!"

Roasted Capon

1 capon (approx. 7 lbs.)
1/2 cup chopped parsley
2 Tbsp. hyssop
2 Tbsp. rosemary
2 Tbsp. chopped sage
4 eggs, hard boiled
1/4 cup currants
1 tsp. salt

Take some of the fat from the inside of the capon - about 1/2 cup - and chop it as finely as possible. Mix with parsley, hyssop, rosemary, and sage. Chop eggs well and add to mixture, along with remaining ingredients. Mix well and stuff into capon. Place in covered roasting pan and bake at 350°F until done - approximately 3 hours (use a meat thermometer to ensure proper temperature). Serve hot.

This afternoon as I was taking stock of my root cellar, I came across a small sack of turnips that I had forgotten. Remarkably, they were still in quite good shape, so I roasted them up by the fire, chopped them up, and then cooked them again, this time in a dish with eggs, cheese, and butter. They made an excellent supper, and with luck there will still be some left over for breakfast tomorrow.

Roasted Turnips

5 medium turnips
1 cup soft cheese, grated
3 eggs
4 Tbsp. butter, melted
1 Tbsp. sugar
1/2 tsp. cinnamon
1/4 tsp. salt

Trim and wash the turnips. Bake in a greased, covered dish until soft - about an hour at 350°F. Let cool and then peel and cut into small strips. Add cheese and set aside.

Beat eggs, sugar, cinnamon, and salt. Pour over turnips and cheese. Add melted butter and mix well. Put into greased pan and bake at 350°F until set - about 35 minutes.

Mid-month. Not sure of the exact date, since I have been feeling a little under the weather with a dreadful head cold. Since most meats this time of year are preserved – salted or smoked – I often find myself craving something fresh. Thus, I turn to the fruits of the waters, and rejoice when I hear the wheels of the fishmonger's cart on the cobbles, bringing succulent treasures from the sea. Oysters and other bivalves come plentiful even in winter, and the creamy base of a stew will stick to my ribs when I am feeling droopy with cold and hunger.

Hopefully, it will raise my spirits as well. I've been feeling out of sorts because I had to fire Merwyn again yesterday evening. He got impertinent with me when I asked him to bait a mouse trap in one of the root cellars. He said the only mouse raiding my stores was me. Of all the cheek!

Oyster Stew

1 pint shucked oysters
4 tablespoons butter
1/2 medium onion, minced
1 small garlic clove, minced
4 cups milk
1/4 cup flour
1/2 tsp. salt
1/4 tsp. white pepper

Clean oysters of sand and any shell pieces.

Melt butter in a large pot, add onions and garlic, and sauté until onions become translucent. Add flour, salt, and pepper and stir until evenly mixed. Slowly add milk, stirring constantly. Bring to a low boil and simmer until thickened. Serve with a splash of sherry.

Smoking Month, 25th day
The cold months of winter are also conducive to making my favorite lemon tart, as the base of lemon and sugar must chill overnight. I can set the mixing bowl well covered in the root cellar, where it will stay cool without freezing, until I am ready to bake. I often mix several batches at once, if I've enough lemons ripe. It is good to have on hand when I've a particular taste for the tart's sour sweetness, or if friends are likely to call for an evening of games and merriment, like "Squeal, Piggy, Squeal" or "Blindman's Wand"

Lemon Tart

2 large lemons, washed
1 cups sugar
1/4 tsp. salt
2 eggs
2 Tbsp. butter, melted
1 Tbsp. flour

Take the zest from the lemons and set aside. Section the lemons, removing the seeds, pith, and membranes, and place in glass mixing bowl. Add sugar and salt, and mix well. Cover and refrigerate for 24 hours, stirring occasionally. In a separate bowl, beat eggs well. Add butter and flour and whisk until frothy. Add to lemon mixture and pour into tart crust and bake at 425°F for 30 minutes. Reduce temperature to 350°F and bake for an additional 20 minutes, or until a knife inserted in the center comes out clean. Let cool, serve at room temperature.

I suspect I got a bit carried away at making wafers last night. This morning I awoke to find that there were no more eggs anywhere to be found in the house, and the shelves in the second pantry are filled with badly wrapped bundles of wafers. Perhaps I shouldn't be storing the wafer iron next to the casks of blackberry mead. Then again, what better way is there to pass a cold winter night?

Wafers

1/2 cup flour
1/3 cup cream
1 egg yolk
1 Tbsp. rose water
3 Tbsp. sugar
pinch cinnamon
pinch salt

Mix ingredients together well. Spoon out into a wafer (or pizzelle) maker and cook to desired doneness. The wafers will keep for weeks in a sealed, airtight container.

"Tilling Month" (February)

Tilling Month is the time to maintain the beds and prepare them with hay and compost for the season to come. Work a second time the soil in readiness for planting.

~East Riding Horticultural Society Manual - Volume 4~

Tilling Month, 12ᵗʰ day
I truly loathe this time of year. There is always so much work to be done in the garden and it is so much work to make sure Merwyn does it correctly. This afternoon I had to tell him three times to turn the soil over withershins to keep the weeds confounded. At least the olitory is done now, though if it weren't such a bother I'd go out with a spade and give it an extra turn.

The days are slowly growing long. Yet, I find myself with many hours when the garden cannot hold my attention. Once the beds are worked, the compost turned and worked into the soil, there is little more I can do outside, and even the greenhouses do not require my whole day's work. Thus, I find myself devoting more time to knife and kettle than to hoe and spade. While I set about making duck in a piquant sauce, Merwyn suggested I try his Mam's recipe for another type of compote – a way to use up the bits and pieces of stored vegetables which remain at the end of winter.

[Editor's Note: This entry allowed us to appropriately place one of the extra pages written in a different hand. We have reproduced the recipe as closely as possible, given that the handwriting was not nearly as neat or precise as Harald's and the spelling was somewhat problematic. Additionally, Merwyn's 'Mam' seems a frugal sort, the recipe was written on the back of a sheet of paper, which looks to be one page of a long letter from a distant relation.]

Pickled Duck

1 lb. duck
1 medium onion, finely chopped
2 Tbsp. olive oil (approx.)
1/2 cup chicken broth
1/2 cup red wine
1/2 tsp. cinnamon
1/2 tsp. ginger
1 tsp. mustard
salt and pepper to taste

Slice the duck meat into large pieces and sauté in olive oil, adding salt and pepper as desired. Remove from pan and set aside, along with the drippings. Sauté onion in olive oil, cooking until tender. Add broth, wine, and cinnamon. Return duck with drippings to the pan and bring to a boil. Remove from heat and add mustard.

Ate the last of the compote at lunch. Strange that I remember loving it so just a few weeks back when it was new, but now I think I'd like to feed the lot of it to the pigs. It's still good, mind you. I'm just tired of seeing crocks of it in the cellar.

Compote (Pickled Root Vegetables)

3 parsley roots
3 parsnips
3 carrots
10 radishes
2 turnips
1 small cabbage
1 pear
1/2 tsp. salt
1 cup vinegar
1/4 tsp. pepper
1 cup sweet wine
1/2 cup honey
1 Tbsp. mustard
1/2 cup currants
1 tsp. cinnamon
1/2 tsp. ginger
1/4 tsp. cinnamon
1/8 tsp. cloves
1/8 tsp. nutmeg
1 tsp. anise seed
1 tsp. fennel seed

Peel vegetables and chop them into bite-sized pieces. Parboil them until just tender, adding pears about halfway through cooking time. Remove from water, place on towel, sprinkle with salt, and allow to cool. Then put vegetables in large bowl and add pepper, saffron, and vinegar. Refrigerate for several hours. Then put wine and honey into a saucepan, bring to a boil, and then simmer for several minutes, removing any scum that forms on the surface. Let cool and add currants and remaining spices. Mix well and pour over vegetables. Serve cold.

Heather sent me a present today, a basket of oysters, left from a wagonload delivered yesterday. I think a pie will go down nicely, paired with a dish of pickled beets, buttered bread and some stewed apples. If it turns out well then I'll invite her around for supper tomorrow and make it again. Though I'll have to remember to ask her to bring another basket.

Oyster Pie

4 cups shucked oysters
2 cups white wine
2 cups water
2 Tbsp. butter, melted
1/2 tsp. pepper
1/2 tsp. marjoram
1/2 tsp. oregano
1/4 tsp. nutmeg
1/2 tsp. salt
1 orange, sliced

Pastry for double-crust pie

Boil oysters briefly in wine and water. Strain, place in a mixing bowl with butter and spices, and mix well. Place mixture in bottom crust, with a layer of orange slices in the middle. Add top crust and bake at 350°F until crust is golden.

Ma always told me stewed lentils were the worst dish. She hated cooking them, said it took days to get the smell out of the house. Da and I loved them though, so she made them often and took care to pass on the recipe. Nowadays I don't cook lentils often as they tend to give me the wind. Maybe they did with Da as well. That would explain a lot since I never notice any smell when cooking them.

Lentil Stew

2 Tbsp. olive oil
1 small onion, chopped
2 carrots, chopped
6 cups vegetable broth
2 cups lentils
1 tsp. ginger
1/2 tsp. cinnamon

Sauté the carrot and onion in the olive oil until it starts to soften. Add broth, lentils, and spices. Simmer 1/2 hour or until lentils are soft. Serve poured over sliced bread.

Fat capons are available throughout the year, so I will often boil or roast two or three at a time, just to have a supply of cooked meat to pull apart and heat in my favorite sauces. It's such lovely meat, almost like the bird has been feasting on butter. Of course I think it's best with a creamy, spiced sauce of milk and cloves. That makes such a warm, hearty lunch or supper on days when the snow and cold keep me penned up inside.

Capon in Sauce

1 lb. chicken, cooked
1 cup milk
4 tsp. flour
1/4 tsp. cinnamon
1/8 tsp. mace
1/8 tsp. cloves
pinch saffron
2 eggs, hard boiled

Cut the chicken into bite-sized pieces and set aside. Melt butter in a large pot, whisk in flour and spices. Slowly whisk in milk. Heat on low until sauce thickens and starts to bubble. Add chicken and stir gently until heated through. Serve with chopped hard-boiled eggs as a garnish.

Winds Month (March)

The month of Winds passes quickly in the anticipation of the coming Spring. It is a time for much work – sowing the flax and grains as well as legumes and herbs, planting nuts and the stones of diverse fruits.

Turn again the beds which have lain fallow the year, and dress the kitchen gardens for the start of the new season.

~East Riding Horticultural Society Manual - Volume 4~

Before the month of winds is half past, I find myself restless for the true start of Spring. My mouth waters for the taste of fresh greens. My toes itch to feel soil beneath them that is neither wet nor chilled, but warm and well-turned. While my pantries are well-stocked with an assortment of dried or housed fruits, pickled and stored vegetables, there is nothing quite like the smell and taste of produce fresh from the ground. The leaner time of year also means I need to think longer to keep my menus varied and interesting. I often find myself standing for more than a quarter hour at a time in one pantry or another, pondering the best combinations of dishes and spices. At least fresh fish is available. The call from the road of a passing fishmonger drew me from my contemplation, and the acquisition of a large piece of fine-fleshed white fish turned my thoughts to an especially filling winter tart.

Fish Pie

6 figs
1/8 cup raisins
1 cup red wine
1 - 2 lbs. fish
1 apple, peeled, cored, and finely chopped
1/2 tsp. cinnamon
1/4 tsp. ginger
1/8 tsp. cloves
1/8 tsp. mace
1/8 cup pine nuts

Pastry for double-crust pie

Boil figs and raisins in wine until tender. Drain them, grind with a mortar and pestle (or food processor) and set aside. Grind the fish until smooth and mix with the figs and raisins and remaining ingredients. Place in pie shell and cover with top crust. Bake at 350°F until done - about 1 hour.

I thought up something new for supper this evening. I cooked up a sauce of raisins and spices, made sweet with honey and biting with vinegar. Served over fish, it was very pleasant indeed! I must remember to tell Heather about it the next time I'm down at the Turnip. I'm sure she'd be interested.

Fish in Raisin Sauce

4 perch fillets
1/2 cup red wine
1/2 cup water
1/2 cup raisins
1/8 cup honey
1/4 tsp. ginger
1/8 tsp. cinnamon
1/8 tsp. cloves
1/2 slice bread, ground
olive oil
salt
pepper
mace

Rinse perch fillets, place in a baking dish, and bake at 350°F for 15-20 minutes.

Grind raisins with a mortar and pestle or food processor into a paste. Place into a saucepan along with wine, water, bread crumbs, and fine spice powder and bring to a boil. Reduce to medium heat and simmer for about 20 minutes.

Remove the fish from the baking dish and pan-fry it in olive oil for about 10 minutes. Sprinkle with salt, pepper, and mace to taste. Serve hot topped with the wine sauce.

The extended cold of the past fortnight allowed the wagons to come further than usual from the sea, and I was able to get several pounds of scallops, some of which I have packed on ice in the deep cellars. They should hold for several days, though knowing myself, I doubt they will last that long. These small, sweet treasures of the sea have always been a particular favorite. Merwyn likes them simply fried in butter; I prefer to add a bit more spice.

Scallops

1/2 pound sea scallops (large)
2 Tbsp. green onions, chopped
1 Tbsp. olive oil
pinch ginger and cinnamon
pinch salt
2 slices bread
1/2 cup verjuice
1 clove garlic

Tear bread into pieces and place in a small bowl. Add garlic and verjuice, and stir until mixed. Allow to sit until the bread turns to mush, then strain the liquid into a small saucepan and discard the solids. Bring to a low boil and simmer until thick, stirring constantly.

Sauté onions and scallops in olive oil. Place onto serving plate, cover with sauce, and sprinkle with spices. Serve hot.

If verjuice is unavailable, substitute 1/4 cup lemon juice and 1/4 cup grape juice.

Winds Month, 18ᵗʰ day
I was feeling a bit low this morning. I'm sure it was because of the dream last night where I was a fish and I got caught for Oddy Greenfallow's table. Perhaps I should not eat so much garlic and onions late at night. To improve my mood I decided to bake a simple cheese tart like mum used to make. Nothing cheers one up like a slice of cheese, eggs, and onion! It turned out nicely, all golden on top, though I did use up most of my supply of eggs and butter. I expect I will have to go to the village market this afternoon to replenish my stores. The Greenfallow's cheese is the best, of course, but I'm not sure I will be able to look him in the eye without shrieking. I guess I'll have to buy from Norb Fenchurn instead. More's the pity as he thinks very highly of his products.

Cheese Tart

1 medium onion, finely chopped
6 eggs
1/2 lb. (2 cups) mozzarella, grated
2 Tbsp. butter
1/2 tsp. salt

Pastry for single-crust pie

Beat eggs, add other ingredients, and pour into an unbaked pie crust. Bake at 350°F until lightly browned on top - about an hour. Serve hot or cold.

Knowing I face a long morning working in the chill of not yet spring, Merwyn having quit, again, after my suggestions about ways to improve his Mother's compote recipe, I determined to fortify myself with a hot breakfast. Merwyn has become far too unpredictable. Perhaps his cousin Gilfred would be willing to come work for me.

I call this dish Pochee, since it is served over poached eggs. Heather at the Green Turnip serves something similar she calls "Goldenrod", though she flavors hers with saffron rather than borage. She says the color of the eggs and spices make her think of the wildflowers. She even suggested I bring her some this summer so we can compare the two.

Pochee

2 egg yolks
1/2 cup milk
1 Tbsp. sugar
1/2 tsp. ginger
borage flowers
pinch salt

In a small saucepan, whisk together egg yolks, sugar, and spices. Add milk and whisk well. Place the pan over medium heat and cook, stirring constantly. Remove from heat when the sauce is thick and just starting to boil. Serve hot over poached eggs.

The beets are all a good size now, so this morning I set Gilfred to pulling them up. It's a pity that he has all the wits of a tree stump though. At first he was going to put them in the basket all caked with dirt. I asked him to leave as much dirt as possible in my garden rather than in the house. It took him a moment of pained thought before he smiled and nodded. Then the fool pulled up two more beets and started to vigorously beat them together. I would love to see what would happen if I asked him to clean some eggs! After some gentle correction he managed to get the rest pulled up. I'll roast some of them this evening and eat them with some goat cheese, but the rest will need to be pickled. Maybe I can get Gilfred to pull up some horseradish as well for that.

Preserved Beetroot

6 beets
1/4 cup finely chopped horseradish
1/2 cup honey
1 Tbsp. cumin
2 tsp. salt
1 tsp. pepper
2 cups malt vinegar
2 cups water

Pint jars for canning

Peel beets and steam until just tender. Allow to cool and then slice about 1/4 inch thick. Layer in clean canning jars with horseradish. Mix honey, water, and spices in a saucepan, bring to a boil, and simmer for 15 minutes. Pour into jars over vegetables to cover and screw on lids. Store in refrigerator for one week before serving.

INDEX OF RECIPES

Sweets

Beverages

AFTERWORD

Merwyn left me this morning. Again. I'm not certain what set him off this time. When I came out after luncheon, he was hard at work at the never ending task of weeding. He was using a small, forked trowel, trying to eradicate the dandelions proliferating about the lilacs and lavender. He is quite diligent at his work, and I complimented him on his thoroughness in unearthing the roots.

"I don't know why nature insists on making so many of these," he commented.

"They are prolific," I commented.

"Oh, aye," he seemed to agree. "They're pretty enough, I grant you, scattered across a fallow field. But there's not a blessed thing you can do with 'em."

"On the contrary," I stated, sounding perhaps more vehement than I intended in my efforts to broaden his knowledge. "They make a fairly palatable wine. And the greens, dressed with good, mild oil are tasty in a salad. You can even wilt them with hot bacon fat and salt as you would lettuce or cabbage."

I stopped my dissertation as I realized Merwyn was looking up at me, his expression incredulous. "Well, you can," I stressed.

"Weeds!" he expostulated.

"Tasty weeds," I countered.

"Next thing you'll have me replanting the blasted things!"

I paused, thinking about that. Perhaps they could be controlled if we cultivated them. I know Elwynd Brewer at the tavern makes dandelion wine. He might trade for a steady supply. I came out of my thoughts at an exasperated harrumph from Merwyn.

"Don't want to eat 'em, and I sure fire don't want to grow 'em." And with that he stalked through the gate, letting it slam behind him, leaving his tools where they lay. He set off down the lane at a trot, and no amount of calling would bring him back.

I suppose I shall have to get another lad.